UNDERSTANDING YOUR CREATIVITY

Discover the Internal and External Factors that Affect Your Creative Life

Heidi Thorne

INTRODUCTION: WHY IS BEING CREATIVE SO HARD?

Have you ever said or asked:

Why don't people accept my creative work?

My creative path isn't going as I had hoped or planned.

Why am I struggling with my creativity?

My creative work is horrible. Just look at all these other talented people!

I'm getting no joy out of being creative anymore.

I feel like I'm working hard creatively, and getting nothing from it.

I just can't seem to get creative work done.

All the demands of my life, including the financial ones, are cramping my creativity.

Shouldn't I be getting paid more for my creative work?

If you have, then this book is for you.

The dictionary definition of creativity suggests that it's the ability and process of being creative, as well as that which transcends the traditional to create something original or progressive. That's pretty straightforward. But creativity is far, far from being straightforward. I find it difficult to define, and realize that it is defined in so many ways. We tend to think of creativity as a totally personal internal game, not giving enough credence to the external forces that influence our creative lives.

What follows are my thoughts on the factors that impact creativity based on my personal experience and my observation of others who have pursued a creative path. Note that we'll refer to people who do creative work as "creatives" throughout the book, regardless of whether they do something in the arts or simply approach their work creatively.

You'll find this very different from other books on creativity that offer impractical or cliché creativity tips such as brainstorming, getting out in nature, or learning to meditate. Sure, those kinds of things are amazing activities, and if they work for improving your creativity, great. But I've always found if I have to force myself to do them to spur creativity, I feel awkward, anxious, and definitely not creative. Then I go back to being who I really am.

I will not be talking about how to be creative or more creative. My hope in writing this book is that you will discover, accept, and manage the factors that affect your creativity so that you can fulfill your creative destiny.

It just so happens that they all start with the letter "c."

CHAPTER 1: COMPASS

Many people don't understand their motives when it comes to creativity. Then they wonder why they're not fulfilled. Problem is they haven't determined their motivational compass.

Let's look at the motivations that can determine the direction of your creative life. I've lumped them into two primary categories: expression and external rewards. Both will no doubt resonate with you in some way. But one will certainly be stronger than the other. The one that is stronger should drive your creative life and will determine how much satisfaction you get from it.

Expression. Do you have some ideas or feelings that you feel you must get out of your head and heart and into the world? What you create may or may not be understood or accepted by others, but you don't really care. Maybe you experiment with lots of different creative endeavors because satisfying your curiosity fires you up. You do whatever you do for the pure pleasure of doing it, or to achieve some sort of release for your pent up creative energy. You may also want to have control over the creative process without having to bend to client whims. Notice that all these are focused on your internal thoughts and feelings.

External Rewards. You may be hesitant to say that you want attention, praise, money, appreciation, or connections from being creative. Don't be! The only thing that is wrong with wanting external rewards for your creativity is not recognizing or accepting that you are driven by them.

I didn't just pick these two seemingly opposite forces randomly. Looking at the results of my 2018 Thorne Self Publishing Survey which polled 163 self published authors, the top two overall responses for what motivates them to write and self publish books were "I LOVE writing!" (53.24% of respondents) and "Self expression and creativity" (51.80%), both internal expression motivators.

"Make money from book sales and royalties" ranked 4th overall (45.32%) and "Motivating and offering help and encouragement to others" ranked 6th (34.53%). Money is obviously an external motivator. Even motivating and offering help is external because without others, there would be on one to help.

For this group of surveyed creatives, internal rewards from expression seemed to be the winning motivation, though not by a huge margin. Let's see how this plays itself out in a real world situation.

Those who pursue creative work to earn money—an external reward—are often torn between doing custom work for hire for clients and selling their own expressive work direct to customers. I've done both.

I have the most difficult time being a writer for hire. I had a blogging assignment that allowed me a pretty high degree of creative freedom, along with a byline. While it was lucrative, I still found it frustrating. I'd rather just write what I want and self publish it. If no one likes it, I understand. I'll just keep putting my work out there for those who like what I do. Even though I like getting paid for my creative work, I'm more motivated by expression than external rewards.

You may think that being equally motivated by both expressive and external rewards might be ideal. But I think it creates a great deal of stress because you're always having to decide between the two forces. You'll be chasing every single creative opportunity which will overtax your energy and resources.

Be honest with yourself about what drives you.

Just as creative motivations can be internal or external, there are both internal and external factors that influence our creativity. In the following discussions, notice the tension and impact of internal versus external forces.

CHAPTER 2:
CAPABILITIES

In college, I had to choose an elective to fulfill my communications minor. I choose something along the lines of Art 101. I figured it would be an easy class, compared to the rest of the classes that semester.

Day one: The professor instructs us to go back to our dorm rooms, draw a bunch of things from the room, and come back in an hour. Well, I wasn't living on campus, so doing dorm room drawing wasn't going to happen. But more than that, I can't draw very well. Seriously, I can't. And I don't like doing it either.

So what did I do? As soon as we were released for our dorm room drawing assignment, I marched myself down to the registrar's office and switched my elective to sociology. That was a class I thoroughly enjoyed. Even today, I still enjoy books, blogs, and television shows on social science and history topics. I knew that drawing wasn't for me, and I'm always glad I made that switch.

I also can't write fiction, and don't read much of it either. However, I am constantly in awe of writers who can create characters, plots, dialogue, and settings for novels and screenplays. How do they do it?

Even though I don't possess a lot of the typical creative

skills, I still consider myself creative because, as defined in the beginning, I can think and write in original and progressive ways. People like scientists, athletes, healthcare workers, and moms are also creative thinkers. Often they have to be! Creative capability is more than the arts and music.

Recognize, too, that when you feel you can't or don't want to pursue something, you may be defining what creative paths are not for you. Save your energy for the pursuits that matter to you and that leverage your capabilities.

CHAPTER 3: COMFORT

If you follow authors and writers on social media, you'll see so many of them posting about their coffee. Seriously, they do! They show photos of their mugs, often emblazoned with clever quotes or quips, noting how coffee is what fuels their creativity.

In addition to those displaying their home brewed cups, others post pictures of themselves at their "coffices," the coffee shops-cum-offices where they proudly state that they get a lot of work done. I can totally relate! I do my very best writing and flesh out many ideas while working at these places, even though I drink tea instead of coffee.

So is it the caffeine in the coffee or tea? Well, caffeine as a creativity booster is hotly and scientifically debated, both for and against. What I think could foster home and coffee shop creativity for many is that both venues can be comfort zones. Comfort zones. Yes, the negative term people use for when things are comfortable physically, emotionally, or intellectually, and you're not willing to try something new.

But I have a different definition. I think comfort zones can be creative zones. Imagine how creative you would be if you had to rethink your morning routines every single morning. What if you had to be in a new setting every single day? Here's how I got a taste of what that's like.

While working my way through college and graduate school, I did a fair amount of temporary administrative assistant work. It can be very disorienting. You're trying to figure out a new landscape with every single assignment. New commute route. New people. Working in an office that belongs to someone else. You have to figure out the most basic of things, like where the bathrooms are, how lunchtime works, and where to stash your stuff. You know how to do the work, but you're working on a different computer set up for someone else's preferences. I didn't know the office politics either, but it was often obvious what was going on.

That was certainly not a comfort zone. Even if most of these assignments were positive experiences overall and the people were very pleasant, my creative energy during that time was zapped. I was exhausted from handling life management issues, leaving little energy, especially mental energy, for creative pursuits or even creative thinking.

So I think there's a case for establishing your own comfort zones where the familiarity or desirability of physical place and routine can free up your energy to focus on more creative work. I've set up a personal routine that includes blocks of "comfort zone" time and place to concentrate on creativity. It works for me and might for you, too.

CHAPTER 4: CHAOS

Went to a conference held in a facility designed to develop creativity. It was filled with a jumble of bright colors, a mix of furniture styles and sizes, and all kinds of playthings, books, and art supplies. But this wasn't a place for kids. It was for adults. The theory was that you were in a different and fun environment that could foster new ideas and conversations.

Sounds like fun, right? Well, I found it to be the most uncomfortable of environments and couldn't wait to leave. I couldn't concentrate on the conversations I was having with fellow attendees. Maybe it was because we were all on different chairs which put us on different levels, literally and figuratively. Rather than fostering creativity, it felt more like chaos, or being at a circus.

People often connect chaos with creativity. For some people, an overload of sensory stimuli can help them make mental or emotional connections that help them do creative work. They also can't be bothered with keeping their workspaces in order because they're constantly churning out new creations. Some may even quickly or impulsively hop from one creative outlet to another. They're neophiliacs, constantly needing novelty to fuel their creative spirits.

For others, like me, chaotic external environments are overwhelming, stopping the ability to do any work, creative or otherwise. I need as uncluttered an environment as possible to concentrate on the activity at hand. I also need to concentrate on something for an extended period of time before I decide that I've had enough of it.

Recognize and respect your level of comfort with chaos. Neither end of the spectrum is right or wrong. It's what works for you. Again, it's all about your comfort zone.

CHAPTER 5: CHOICES

Unfortunately, creativity is often linked with obsession. We've romanticized the image of the starving artist or reclusive genius who has intentionally sacrificed everything for their passion, and we marvel at their accomplishments. But is that level of commitment required to be creative?

Creativity is about choices and values. Starving artists have chosen and value their work over food, health, and finances. Reclusive geniuses have made a similar choice about relationships. Those are extreme cases of an internal creative compass.

True, there may be occasions where your creative work may take priority over standing commitments to yourself and others. The emphasis here is on occasions. But when it becomes a habit, or you start to shun all your real life commitments, you may be bordering on obsession. Obsessive behaviors are usually a symptom of other things going on in your life. Then you have to ask yourself if you're trying to escape commitments, using creativity as an excuse.

You might think that equally dividing time, resources, energy, and attention between your creative work and your real life might be the solution to achieve balance and avoid obsession. It isn't. By artificially divvying up your commitments to both your internal expressive needs and the needs of your external world, you might not commit fully to any part of your life, which could lead to feeling guilty or dissatisfied. Flexibility to meet the most important and shifting needs is the key.

You may also be choosing to be distracted by minor things such as your electronic devices or social media. This is both an obsession and a dividing of time and attention. Like obsession, paying attention to the less significant could be an escape from something you don't want to do or face. And like dividing time, it lowers the energy and time you commit to anything, which can lead to dissatisfaction with everything.

If you find your finances, health, relationships, and productivity starting to suffer, or you're feeling dissatisfied with your creative work, it might be time to get some outside perspective on your life and work choices with coaching or counseling.

CHAPTER 6: CASH

We'd like to think cash doesn't matter when it comes to creativity. But it does. How will you finance your creative adventures?

Since ancient times, artists, authors, and even scientists have been sponsored by patrons. Paradoxically, creatives want the freedom from financial worries that sponsorship provides so they can freely express themselves, yet sponsors may have expectations for quality, quantity, or even content of work. This is a perfect example of the problem of having equal expression and external reward motivations that I talked about earlier.

Patronage by the rich or royal might still be done, but today creatives are seeking support from regular people on the Internet who are willing to pay a few dollars for subscriptions or donations. In theory, this sounds ideal. Unfortunately, in practice, this model is very challenging.

There are creatives who are willing to become their own patrons by sponsoring their own creative adventures, sometimes even to their detriment. For example, I run across hopeful first-time authors who think that their first foray into self publishing will set them up financially. Sadly, as I found from my self publishing surveys, the statistics aren't in their favor. Yet they're often willing to spend a lot of cash to make their impossible dreams come true, even though they may never make back their investment through book sales.

Some creative expression is expensive to pursue, too. An example would be large metal sculptures which have high material, production, and workspace costs.

Creatives who are more motivated by external rewards might finance their creativity by doing creative work for customers.

So how willing are you to sacrifice your financial well-being or future to achieve your creative dreams? On the other hand, are you willing to adjust your creative aspirations to match your financial limitations and obligations? Will you seek the support of patrons? Or will you surrender your expressive motivations to finance your lifestyle through creative work for customers? Your choices will determine what creative goals you can achieve, and how and when you pursue them.

CHAPTER 7: CURVES

I didn't know what to say. I was just hoping that my friend didn't see my shoulders and expression go limp as she described her new business idea. It wasn't that it was a bad idea. It was just about a decade too late for the market, or, as some would say, "behind the curve."

What is the curve? If the sales of a product or service over time were graphed on x and y axes, it will typically create a bell-shaped curve. Sales in the early "ahead of the curve" stage are low, continue to grow upwards to a peak growth level, then eventually decline to levels similar to the product introduction, maybe even to zero, in the "behind the curve" stage.

You're probably thinking, "So what does this have to do with creativity?" Actually, a lot, depending on the direction of your creative motivation compass. For creatives who are externally motivated by acceptance and money, understanding the timing issues can help avoid expensive losses or pursuing unfulfilling and unprofitable work.

In the ahead of the curve stage, adoption of a product, service, or concept has low acceptance and sales. It has not yet reached a point of critical mass where many sales can occur. Avant-garde art—meaning that which is experimental, radical, or never been done—is an example of ahead of the curve work. The masses may not understand the creator's vision, and be slow to accept and invest in it.

When a product enters the behind the curve stage, acceptance is not a problem, but competition is. If sales of the product or idea has achieved some level of success, a myriad of similar competitors will enter the market. Pricing and differentiation become more important and difficult when it comes to selling, which usually means a bigger investment in advertising and marketing. This was the market situation that my friend would have be entering. From what I knew of her intended market, it would have been a losing proposition right from the start.

At both ends of the sales curve, only dedicated fans and followers are making up the market. These are often referred to as niche markets. An ahead of the curve niche could grow, but a behind the curve niche will be static or decrease. Some niche markets have a very flat bell curve distribution. These niche markets start out slow or low, don't grow much, and then decline. Some believe that there are riches in underserved niche markets. But the key to reaching niche markets is building a dedicated fan base. That could take an investment of time, effort, and money.

Analysis and research of market and Internet traffic trends will also be required. Sorry, I know that's not what creatives want to hear. If that's not a skill you have, you might need to get some outside help to teach you the skills or do this for you. Sometimes being non-creative is the best way to help you be creative.

CHAPTER 8:
CHANGE

Is there some creative activity that you used to be good at, but don't do now? I have a list. One thing I used to do during my corporate career was make a lot of my work clothes. It was personal expression both in making and wearing them. I can't even imagine doing that now. What changed? I did. My life did.

Life stages and changes can have a huge influence on creativity. They can turn something that used to provide a great amount of satisfaction into a waste of valuable time and energy. Conversely, these changes can spark or revive other creative pursuits.

You may grieve at the loss of interest in your past creative activities. You may be a bit angry at yourself for investing so much in something that means so little to you now. And what will your family, friends, and clients think about your shift in pursuits, priorities, or attitudes? Who are you now anyway?

Some people are so concerned about their image, or salvaging the investment they dumped into previous endeavors, that they will continue to pursue old interests even if they're mentally and emotionally checked out. Changing what doesn't serve you is an act of creative courage.

Realize, too, that there may be times in your creative life, where you'll reach a natural plateau. You've figured out what works for you in terms of creative effort and what you get in return from doing it. You're efficient at what you do, and might even have a high output or quality of work. If you sell your work, the market for it may be stable, even if it's not growing.

But how do you know if and when you should move from a plateau? I've noticed that when a change is coming or needed, I start feeling anxious, although that might be my paranoia when things are going good. But at least it gets me thinking about what's next. Maybe you'll feel bored. You might also find yourself intentionally ignoring important signals, like a dieter who refuses to get on the scale to monitor her weight. Or people and things in your environment might seem to be out of whack somehow while you're blissfully rolling along.

At other times, changes in your outer world could force you to change your creative focus or commitment. Finances, family issues, the economy, health, or distractions as random as remodeling your home could all derail your creativity. While we'd like to think that our love for whatever we do should help us power through any challenges, that is unrealistic.

Recognize and accept that your creative journey could take detours, completely grind to a halt, and then take on new or unexpected directions. Accepting change is also an act of creative courage.

CHAPTER 9:
CULTURE

How do your family, church, school, and friends view creativity? Does their perspective on it, or their participation in creative work, have an impact on your own personal creativity? I think the influence of others in your community and life can have a significant impact on your creativity or how you express and explore it.

My dad was an extremely talented professional musician. Our home was overrun with all things music. Of course, I was steered into music lessons. Because he did teach others, my dad tried to teach me to play the piano, emphasis on tried. I tried really hard, too, but we both just ended up frustrated. So then I took piano lessons at school with another teacher. I gained some skill, but I never gained a feel for music. Even went into the band in high school and, mercifully, was dismissed from both the band and band class with a failing grade in sophomore year.

I'm just not musically inclined. Just add this to my lack of drawing skills I talked about earlier. One would think that being surrounded with music my entire young life that I might have some advantage or interest in being creative through music. Nope. But I felt there was some expectation that I should pursue music.

Unlike mine, there are other families and communities

where creativity or the arts are not as prized, maybe even discouraged, censored, or prohibited.

Regardless of which end of the creativity spectrum your culture is on, there's no doubt that the prevailing rules and expectations can influence your choice of creative pursuits and how vigorously you pursue them, or even if you pursue them at all.

Does conforming to written or unwritten rules and expectations of your culture cramp or ramp up creativity?

Sometimes conforming to official or unwritten cultural rules can facilitate your creative work, but only if this a culture you truly want to be a part of. Not conforming to its norms may brand you as arrogant or ignorant, or as an outsider or newbie. "He doesn't understand us. He's not one of us. Why should we pay attention to him?" Trust is destroyed and your creative work could have a difficult time reaching this audience.

Ask yourself, too, if you're breaking a cultural rule or norm just for shock value, like a child who misbehaves because she desperately wants her parents' attention. While willful rule breaking will get attention, it will also give you a reputation for being difficult. That is not creative rebellion. That is craving attention.

But there may be situations, like my failed musical endeavors, where walking away from the culture and its rules may be necessary for your creativity and sanity.

The trick is developing the experience, wisdom, and empathy to know when it's appropriate to conform and when to break cultural rules and connections. This takes patience, as well as participation in and with the culture.

CHAPTER 10: CHANCE

Though writing is my primary creative activity today, it wasn't always like that. Through school and college, I could write pretty well, and usually placed in honors English or was able to test out of English classes. But I never really thought of myself as a writer, and never wrote for the fun of it.

But then that all changed when I went back into a sales career after college. Yes, sales. The company I worked for was using some dreadfully dry sales letters. Since it was a peak-and-valley industry, and I needed to fight off boredom, I used the down periods to reinvent those letters into fun or interesting reads. Thus began my writing career, which later led to a marketing manager post writing advertising and press copy, a very long career as a trade newspaper editor and advertising director, and then self publishing several business books. And those later writing-related adventures have their own twisty origin stories.

How did I get to that initial watershed moment when I tackled the first sales letter rewrite? Who could have ever predicted or planned such a situation, or what it would lead to?

Some believe that there's a reason for everything that happens, or that some divine or cosmic force has a hand in it. Regardless of your belief, I think we can all agree that chance events can have a significant impact on our creative paths.

The worst part about chance is that it is the most uncontrollable of the external factors. But we can think of chance as chances, chances to make interesting and courageous choices about our creative path. That is how we can control the uncontrollable.

CHAPTER 11: CONNECTION

While I'm intrigued by poetry, and have made a commitment to read it on a regular basis from a variety of poets, I have to confess that many times I don't understand it. What's even stranger is that a poem written hundreds of years ago might resonate with me more than something that was just published.

Here's why I think some poems are so opaque to me. They include references to the poet's unique and unknown personal experiences, similar to telling an inside joke and wondering why those outside your intimate circle of family and friends don't get it. Or a poem seems to be a stream of consciousness account of a bizarre dream. Everything is out of context and the poem cannot stand by itself without a lot of explanation. These poets are expressing themselves, but not necessarily connecting.

This begs the question of whether creative work needs to communicate with others. This is an issue I bump into frequently in working with authors. When I ask them who will read the books they write, they have no idea. Or they'll say their books are for "everyone." That's the telltale sign they have put no thought into the audience for their work. Then they wonder why no one wants to buy and read their books.

If fostering connection through your creativity isn't important to you, that's fine. You're obeying your internal compass to express yourself in any way that suits you. Just don't get disappointed expecting the external world to accept and reward you and your work.

But if you hope that your creative work will reach the minds and hearts of others, it must communicate in a way that will be understood and appreciated by your intended audience, while still pushing them to the new and different. This is a challenging balancing act that may require a lot of experience, experimentation, and empathy.

CHAPTER 12:
COHORTS

"This will be a group project." How I dreaded hearing those words when I was in school, and later in my working life. It's not that I don't enjoy people. I love connecting and being with intelligent, fun, and friendly folks. But when it comes to being creative and working, leave me alone!

Then there are others that crave being in groups to produce their best creative work, otherwise they feel lonely and isolated. Or they like the opportunity to bounce off or trade ideas, thereby generating even more ideas. Some may find joy in doing an activity in the company of others. These are definitely creatives who are motivated by the external rewards of connection.

Your need for a creative cohort could determine how, how often, when, and where you pursue your creative endeavors. Work your work around those needs to boost your creative output and satisfaction.

On a different plane of cohort, some writers feel they need a muse, God or gods, or some other external entity or force to feel or be creative. You might even hear them say they've lost their muse when their work quality or output starts to wane.

What I think people sometimes identify as an external

muse, is really just a recognition of their own creative energies. Your energy, both physical and mental, will ebb and flow over time, even within the span of one day. Set up your sacred comfort zones of time and place to leverage your energies.

CHAPTER 13: COMPARISON

Some of my friends are so talented with art, some that you wouldn't even expect to be. Others appear to be raking in big rewards from things like writing or speaking. And I often slipped into thinking, "Why can't I do that?" Or, "Why am I not doing that?"

Then I have to get a grip on myself and realize that I'm falling into the creativity comparison trap. What happens when comparison creeps in is the temptation to veer from our creative strengths by chasing what works for someone else.

There's nothing wrong with observing other creative people for inspiration. It's when inspiration turns into nothing more than imitation and envy that it becomes a problem.

But the comparison doesn't stop there. All of us are our worst critics. This is a different level of comparison trap where we're comparing ourselves to an ideal and unrealistic version of ourselves. As with external comparison, this keeps us from doing the creative work we're uniquely suited to do.

An obsession with perfection is the culprit. Realize, too, that you'll keep ramping up your definition of perfection

www.ingramcontent.com/pod-product-compliance
Lightning Source LLC
Chambersburg PA
CBHW072027280526
45788CB00007B/2703

CHAPTER 14:
GOING FORWARD

As you should have gathered by now, creativity is personally defined by understanding yourself and the environment in which you live and work. Being able to navigate your creative life in a fulfilling way for you may be the most creative thing you'll ever do.

until you've set up an impossible standard, a standard even you, the standard setter, couldn't achieve.

Better to think in terms of best possible and always getting better, not perfection.